close

A JOURNEY IN SCOTLAND

For Jim and Pat Pollok-Morris

First published by Northfield Print,
www.northfieldprint.co.uk, on the occasion
of the exhibition 'close' at the Royal Botanic
Garden Edinburgh, 27 September 2008
– 11 January 2009 and Bonhoga Gallery,
Shetland, 14 February 2009 – 15 March 2009.

Printed and bound by Printer Trento, Italy.

Designed by Drew Creative.

www.drewlondon.co.uk

ISBN
978-0-9560338-0-2

Contents

Foreword: Sir Roy Strong FSA., FSRL.   9
Introduction: Allan Pollok-Morris   10-13

54° N 5° W   Jim Buchanan   16-23
              Labyrinths, Sandyhills, Dumfriesshire
55° N 3° W   Andy Goldsworthy   26-37
              Works in Dumfriesshire and
              National Museum of Scotland Edinburgh
              Charles Jencks   38-45
              The Garden of Cosmic Speculation,
              Dumfriesshire. Landform UEDA
              Gallery Of Modern Art, Edinburgh
              Maggie's Highlands Cancer Caring Centre
              garden, Raigmore Hospital, Inverness
              Zara Milligan   46-53
              Dunesslin, Dumfriesshire
              Alec Finlay   54-61
              WW Letterboxes, Cairnhead Community
              Forest, Dumfriesshire
              Xylotheque, The Hidden Gardens, Glasgow
4°W   Douglas Coltart MLI., MSGD.   62-67
              New Lanark Roof Garden and
              private garden Ayrshire
55.5° N 3° W Ian Hamilton Finlay 1925 - 2006   70-81
              Little Sparta, Lanarkshire
4° W   Rolf Roscher and Chris Rankin   82-87
              The Hidden Gardens, Glasgow
              James Alexander Sinclair   88-93
              Mount Stuart, Isle of Bute
6° W   Peter Cool   94-100
              Jura House, Isle of Jura

Contents

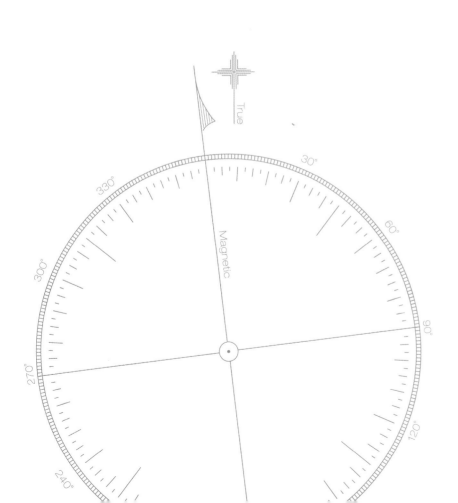

56° N 2°W **Catherine Erskine & Elliot Forsyth** 102-109
Cambo House, Fife

4°W **Jinny Blom** 110-119
Corrour Lodge Gardens, by Fort William

Niall Manning & Alastair Morton 120-125
Dun Ard, Stirlingshire

6° W **Penelope Hobhouse Hon.D.Litt. M.A.** 126-131
The Monks Garden, Inner Hebridean island

57° N 2°W **Mary Ann Crichton Maitland** 134-139
Daluaine, Aberdeenshire

Dr. Thomas Smith 140-145
Rubislaw Den North, Aberdeen

3° W **Angelika, Dowager Countess Cawdor** 146-153
Cawdor Castle and Gardens, Nairn

4°W **Gerald Laing** 154-159
Kinkell, Ross & Cromarty

58°N 3°W **Xa Tollemache** 162-171
Dunbeath, Caithness

60°N **'close' exhibition** 175
Bonhoga Gallery, Lerwick, Shetland
14 February 2009 – 15 March 2009

Acknowledgements 176

Foreword
Sir Roy Strong FSA., FSRL.

This collection of photographs by Allan Pollok-Morris is a hymn to the Scottish garden, although some gardens gathered here are not the work of Scots. Nor is this introduction, although it is by someone who, like the gardeners here, recognises that horticulture North of the Border has a distinctive life of its own. Nearly all who have written record the overwhelming impact of the terrain and of a climate harsher and more unsparing of those who war against it.

Allan Pollok-Morris catches the quintessential qualities which set Scottish gardens and gardening apart. He records the sense of struggle in a land where the forces of nature always threaten to defeat those who set out to defy it and to tame and cultivate. His pictures respond fully to the massive, gaunt, if verdant landscape and to the amazing permutations of light from skies which can range from being bright and tranquil to ones which are troubled and turbulent. And they of course in turn affect the whole vision of the garden, one in which the appearance of flowers at all calls for celebration. The season is after all short and far later than in the south.

Perhaps, however, what fascinates and pleases me most from this garden gathering is that all of them embrace change with excitement, for horticulture is a mutant art. To that one can add a return to a consideration of gardening in a far more philosophical light. Time and again there is a quest for the rediscovery of meaning in the garden. What is it there for, what does it mean, how does it express the ideas and commitment of its creators. For that return to the great tradition one must be truly grateful.

Introduction
Allan Pollok-Morris

What?

What is the 'close' collection? It is my attempt, through words and images, to capture the works of garden designers, plants people, artists and architects that have been created against the stunning backdrop of the Lowlands, Highlands, and Islands of Scotland.

Why?

Why did I begin? I grew up in Scotland, in the foothills of the Highlands, and have never lost touch with this unique place. Whenever I returned home, I would look at the country through the eyes of a photographer who has had the opportunity to explore landscape design internationally.

The more I explored, the more I became convinced that there was something unique about gardens and land-art north of the border. When a Scotland on Sunday poll in December 2004 voted Ian Hamilton Finlay's garden Little Sparta to be the most important work of Scottish art, it was clear that it wasn't just me who felt that way. So I approached the Royal Botanic Gardens Edinburgh with the outline of this project, my aim being to bring these subjects to a wider audience.

How?

This may have begun as a project, but it rapidly turned into something of an odyssey for me; a single journey comprised of many unique stories. I have presented it with direction, moving from the south of the country to the north. This is not a purely geographical statement. There is something almost spiritual in the progression towards the north. In the book *There Where You Are Not* Glenn Gould is quoted as saying, *'Something really happens to people who go into the north – they become at least aware of the creative opportunity which the physical fact of the country represents and…come to measure their own work and life against that rather staggering creative possibility: they become, in effect, philosophers'.*

Man's relationship with the natural world is at the heart of my photography and with subjects as notable as these it is not for me to interfere. My role is simply to capture light and produce images that allow these inspirational creations to be appreciated by the reader as if they were there themselves. In the words of the garden photographer Andrew Lawson (whose photography of Little Sparta is seen in *Little Sparta* by Jessie Sheeler), *'the best garden makers are artists. So what is a photographer to do? He does not want to superimpose his own art on a garden, which is already a work of art in itself'.* It is therefore appropriate that the creators behind the gardens and land-art in this collection give their own descriptions of the scenes and share some of their thoughts, poetry and creative writing with the reader.

As mentioned above, I spend a lot of time researching in other countries. So, did I find an answer to the question of what is unique about Scotland in terms of gardens and land-art? Why is it that a small, often harsh territory holds such a strong set of examples in this field? That it does so, I hope is documented here. Ultimately, however, the answers are more complex than a few words in this introduction, particularly as they may be different for each reader, but if nothing else, I hope this collection stimulates thought and discussion.

close A JOURNEY IN SCOTLAND

close

No one collective description can be applied to the wide variety of subjects in this group. Instead, when choosing a name, I opted for a small, unassuming word which, in Scottish dialect, was used to describe a landscape so inspirational that heaven seemed closer to earth in that place. For example, I grew up in MacGregor country, where it is said the most famous member of this clan, Rob Roy MacGregor, was buried in Balquidder because he had described the glen as 'close'.

The title is also in tribute to a saying in the documentary profession that an image will be of no worth if the photographer isn't close enough to the subject.

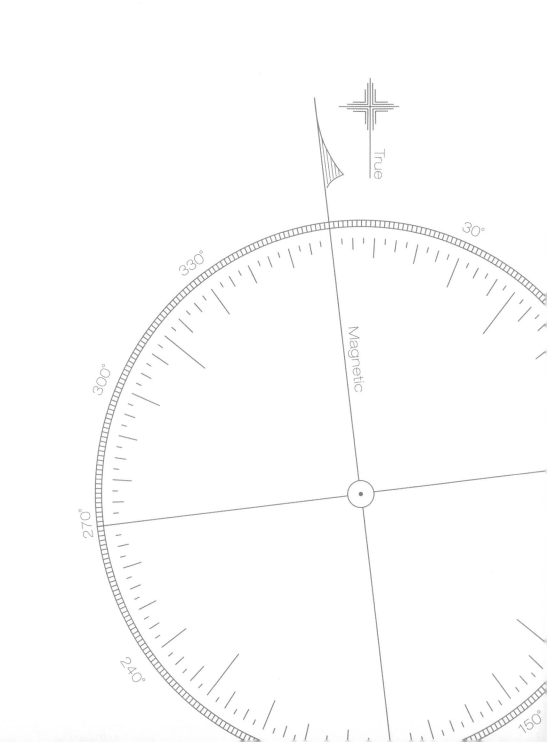

close A JOURNEY IN SCOTLAND

54°N 5°W

Jim Buchanan

Labyrinths, Sandyhills, Dumfriesshire

54°N 5°W

Jim Buchanan
Labyrinths, Sandyhills, Dumfriesshire

Drawing has become an increasingly important language in my creative practise. It begins as a way of articulating a thought; it emerges through a subtle balance between the hand, the eye and brain. Initially I use a free flowing pen or soft pencil on paper. This is a fluid process whereby the development and alteration of an idea run consecutively with the act of realising its form in a drawn medium.

Mark making with a stick or rake in sand on a large scale extends the physical act of drawing. As such the beach is an extension of my studio, which allows 1:1 scale drawings of ideas to be created. The geometry, curves and rhythm of a design are explored then at a realistic scale, allowing fine-tuning to be undertaken, and offering the opportunity to walk around. This testing can be then returned back to a design drawing as amendments.

As a child growing up on the West Coast of Ireland, the boundary of my daily movement was how far I could walk before returning home when hunger kicked in. I was introduced to the labyrinth motif through my parents' work in ceramics. It was not long before I was drawing my own labyrinths on the beach: scratched sand designs, and others with constructed walls to resist the incoming sea. The physical act of drawing, then progressing to making a work that engages with nature's constant flux, had irreversibly captured my imagination.

Every labyrinth has a cadence particular to its dimensions, construction material and location. Drawing a labyrinth to scale in the sand gives me the chance to fine-tune these dimensions, and to develop my internal discussion about its final construction and orientation within the landscape.

The incoming tide adds a tension to the beach location. It focuses my mind on my actions, adds clarity to the thought processes, but is a forgiving medium in that drawn lines are easily amended. In the end, no matter how 'precious' one becomes, the sea will reclaim the space. My labyrinths are constructed for people. So taking my design drawing into a public space brings my creative process into the public realm very early on in a realisation.

For this particular labyrinth design I have a private client in mind. I have been puzzled by their garden's location next to a river – sometimes a gentle stream, sometimes a raging torrent threatening a flood – and how this should relate to the proposed labyrinth. By chance, the best area of dry sand for drawing into was located next to a section of the river Nith cutting its way through the mud and sand heading out to sea at low tide. It was not long before this changed direction and scale, with the incoming tide heading back in fast.

The labyrinth drawing confirmed for me the choice of a strongly circular design, reflecting ripples perhaps, although within the design there are distortions within these. Secondly, the design has two paths to choose from, with a centre accessible straight from the entrance. This gives an element of freedom to the walker to choose their journey, and an opportunity to keep walking with no fixed stopping point. Like the fluidity of water. A small detail fixed in my mind from this is the need to include some held water, perhaps captured in a bowl at the centre. Maybe on a larger scale, the river might be encouraged to sometimes flood the labyrinth and allow the water to be held, emphasising the labyrinths design?

Jim Buchanan is author of "Labyrinths for the Spirit" published by Gaia in 2007.

close A JOURNEY IN SCOTLAND

close A JOURNEY IN SCOTLAND

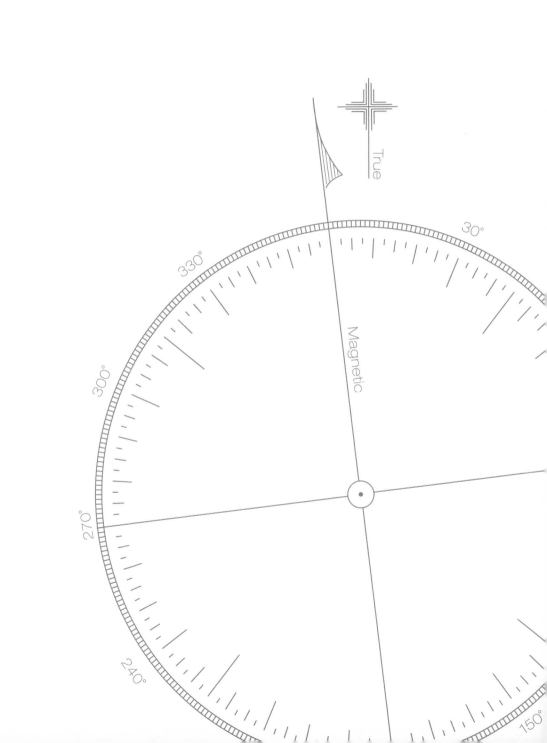

55°N
3°W

Andy Goldsworthy
Works in Dumfriesshire and the
National Museum of Scotland, Edinburgh

Charles Jencks
The Garden of Cosmic Speculation,
Dumfriesshire
Landform UEDA, Gallery of Modern Art,
Edinburgh
Maggie's Highlands Cancer Caring Centre
garden, Raigmore Hospital, Inverness

Zara Milligan
Dunesslin, Dumfriesshire

Alec Finlay
WW Letterboxes, The Hill of Streams,
Cairnhead Community Forest, Dumfriesshire
Xylotheque, The Hidden Gardens, Glasgow

4°W

Douglas Coltart MLI, MSGD
New Lanark Roof Garden
and private garden Ayrshire

Andy Goldsworthy
Works in Dumfriesshire and the National Museum of Scotland Edinburgh

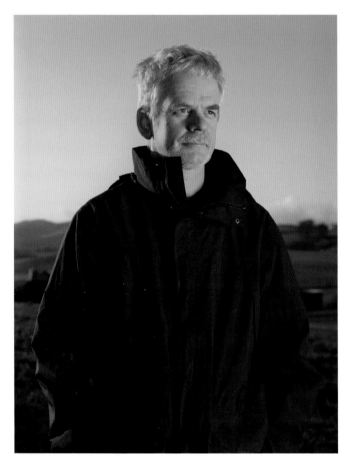

Extracts from Penpont Cairn.

23 December 1999

I have been very anxious about this sculpture and have given enormous thought to its making.

I feel self-conscious about working so prominently in my home place. I will see the resulting sculpture whenever I leave and return to the village. My children will grow up with it. These associations can become rich and beautiful, but if the sculpture does not work then I shall have to live with that. Most artists have to deal at some time with bad reactions from the public, that is normal, but home is where I am most exposed.

I have surprised myself by choosing such a prominent site. I tried to talk myself out of it, but somewhere along the process the self-conscious Andy Goldsworthy was replaced by Andy Goldsworthy the artist whose purpose is to make the strongest possible sculpture. It is an honour and responsibility to have been asked by the village to make a work and I must do all that I can to respond as well as I am able.

22 January 2000

The cairn is taking on its character, and although it is too soon to be certain, I feel a welling up of excitement at how good the form is. I live, work, sleep and breathe this piece at the moment. Stones laid in the day are turned over in my mind in the evening.

It is strange to talk of such hard and heavy work as enjoyable, but the making of this sculpture is the closest I have been with a large stone work to being able to say this. This is due mainly to it being where I live. I go to work as farmers and others are also going to work. I am doing my job as they do theirs. Although the making of a sculpture is obviously out of the ordinary, this particular work has a wonderful sense of the normal and everyday about it.

28 January 2000. The cairn is finished.

It is difficult to describe my feelings. It is far more impressive than I thought it would be. For a work so prominently sited I thought it might be too imposing and appear as if it were shouting for attention in a 'look at me' kind of way. In this instance, however, I am delighted that it should have a strong presence. Standing on the brow of the hill, it appears almost to float. Even I wondered momentarily what is holding it up!

As you walk to the sculpture it changes so much; I like the many different ways in which it can be seen. Of course the form is not perfect, but it has to be the best cairn that I have made so far.

A farmer stopped and when he asked what it was, I explained my ideas of it being a guardian or sentinel to the village. I knew by the tone of my own voice that I was unable to explain fully what the sculpture is about. The farmer stayed for some time and the conversation went from farming to quarries; to things taken away from the land and things given to it; to the standing stones and landmarks in the area and how his young daughter will have the memory of having seen the work being made. Any explanation I can give inevitably falls short of describing the work fully and in many ways it is better described by conversations I had with this man.

Penpont Cairn
Pages 27-28

close A JOURNEY IN SCOTLAND

Scaur Water

Touchstone North
Pages 30-31

The three Cairns at Dunesslin
Pages 32-34

close A JOURNEY IN SCOTLAND

close A JOURNEY IN SCOTLAND

Striding Arches
Pages 35-36

Right
National Museum of Scotland

Charles Jencks
The Garden of Cosmic Speculation

Covering 30 acres in the Borders area of Scotland, the Garden of Cosmic Speculation is conceived as a place to explore certain fundamental aspects of the universe. What are atoms made of and how should we conceive of them? How does DNA make up a living organism and why is it essential to celebrate it in a garden?

The garden uses nature to celebrate nature, both intellectually and through the senses, including the sense of humour. What emerges is a new language of landscape design based on twists and waves, optical illusions, and sudden surprises. It presents a view of the universe quite different from the standard mechanistic model; the complexity sciences show it to be more dynamic and creative than previously conceived.

The garden abstracts this new world view. A water cascade of steps recounts the story of the universe, a terrace shows the distortion of space and time caused by a black hole, a "Quark Walk" takes the visitor on a journey to the smallest building blocks of matter, and a series of sweeping landforms and lakes recall fractal geometry while echoing visually the nearby Scottish Hills.

Landform UEDA. Gallery Of Modern Art, Edinburgh.

This Design, commissioned to enliven a flat lawn and shield noise from the side road, faces two ways: to the gallery and across the road to its sister, the Dean Centre. It's connecting "S" form also derives from two strange attractors discovered by physicists Ueda and Henan. Earth, water and airflows generate wave forms that self-organise around certain attractor basins so there are natural affinities between this shape and the way the earth is moved and people walk. The landform can be used as an open-air gallery.

Maggie's Highlands Cancer Caring Centre garden, Raigmore Hospital, Inverness.

Some day the story of how these Maggie's Centres work and how the architecture and gardens help their healing activity, might be told. But there is an important lesson that we hope to prove in the near future and it relates, if obliquely, to the work going on in the garden, the interactions between DNA and the cells in which it is nurtured.

The Garden of Cosmic Speculation
Pages 39 - 42

close A JOURNEY IN SCOTLAND

Landform UEDA
Gallery Of Modern Art Edinburgh

Left & Right
Maggie's Highlands Cancer Caring Centre garden
Raigmore Hospital, Inverness

Zara Milligan
Dunesslin, Dumfriesshire

There is a wonderful sense of remoteness and timelessness in the surrounding landscape and it is the scale, shape and in part, the wildness of the hills which enhances the intimacy and seclusion of the garden.

This is epitomised by the individual plants. I just love their beauty and seeing them flourish. Finding a little treasure, such as Anemone trullifolia, returning bravely year after year is what really draws me into the garden when the rain is pouring down.

close A JOURNEY IN SCOTLAND

Sculpture by
Judith Gregson

HaHa by Charles Morris

Alec Finlay

WW Letterboxes, The Hill of Streams,
Cairnhead Community Forest, Dumfriesshire
The Woodland Platform and Xylotheque, The Hidden Gardens, Glasgow

Alec Finlay, the Woodland Platform and Xylotheque,
the Hidden Gardens twenty-four hour hyakuin renga

'This is my listening face'

WORLDWIDE LETTERBOXING

Letterboxing is a hybrid form of hobby walking and rubber stamp collecting. Alec is placing 100 letterboxes at sites around the globe (51 have been installed to date). Each box protects a circle poem. Some of the boxes are sited singly, in locations that are described in guides written by their keepers, some are composed in walks.

THE HILL OF STREAMS.
Alec Finlay and Alexander & Susan Maris.

a letterbox walk by way of seven confluences, Cairnhead Community Forest (Scotland).

WWLB037 Where Glenjaan becomes Dalwhat
WWLB038 Where Benbuie becomes Dalwhat
WWLB039 Where Conrick becomes Dalwhat
WWLB040 Where Dibbin becomes Dalwhat
WWLB041 Where Lagdubh becomes Dalwhat
WWLB042 Where Back becomes Dalwhat
WWLB043 Where Fingland becomes Dalwhat
WWLB044 Where Ramscleuch becomes Dalwhat

Hill of Streams
Pages 55-59

The plaque reads:

WWLB041

HILL OF STREAMS
WORLDWIDERUBBERSTAMP
LETTERBOXCIRCLEPOEM

glenjaan burn
dalwhat
dibbin lane
fingland burn
back burn
dalwhat
ramscleuch burn
dalwhat
dalwhat
dalwhat
dalwhat water
dalwhat
dalwhat
lagdubh burn
benbuie burn
conrick burn
dalwhat

close A JOURNEY IN SCOTLAND

Left & Right
The Woodland Platform and Xylotheque
The Hidden Gardens Glasgow

Douglas Coltart MLI, MSGD
New Lanark Roof Garden and private garden Ayrshire

The rich and varied landscape of Scotland provides a wonderful backdrop to its gardens. Designers usually strive to bring a sense of place into their gardens; however in Scotland it is often hard to escape the dramatic character of the landscape that permeates our gardens and our lives.

One of the biggest challenges, when faced with a landscape filtering back towards the house, is restraint. Often the key is to not compete with the surrounding views but to blend seamlessly into them. This does not mean that designs have to be watered down and naturalistic but merely that they do not fight with the landscape. Nor does it mean that 'twee' or boring gardens should rule the day; classic and modern gardens can easily sit within naturalistic spaces, they simply require a careful use of planting, either through colour or species to unite the two.

The weather is never very far away from anyone who has a garden, especially in Scotland. As a designer it is often part of the brief for the garden to mitigate the effects of one extreme or another. Huge volumes of rain or ferocious winds do bring problems with them but they also constrain briefs to such an extent that they require a great deal of thought and consequently often produce more imaginative designs. Even when extremes are not present, the constantly shifting pattern of weather brings an ever-changing dimension to spaces; even when viewed from indoors.

As well as the landscape and weather, it is the owners of the gardens who shape their designs. The best garden designs are achieved by working closely with the owners throughout the design process. Only by understanding what makes a client tick can you design a garden that ticks their boxes. Designing spaces that work for the way in which owners want to live means that you have to gain an insight into the lives of many people. As such, relationships often carry on long after the physical completion of a project; this is one of the nicest things about the job. Garden design clients are a great bunch of people who either love their external environment or tend to be passionate about plants.

The people of Scotland know the benefits of good design and there is a huge appreciation for the landscape. Ultimately, that is what it's all about. It is never to impose and stamp a garden into a space and onto its owners. It is to work with them and their surroundings to create spaces that are loved.

New Lanark Roof Garden
Pages 63-65

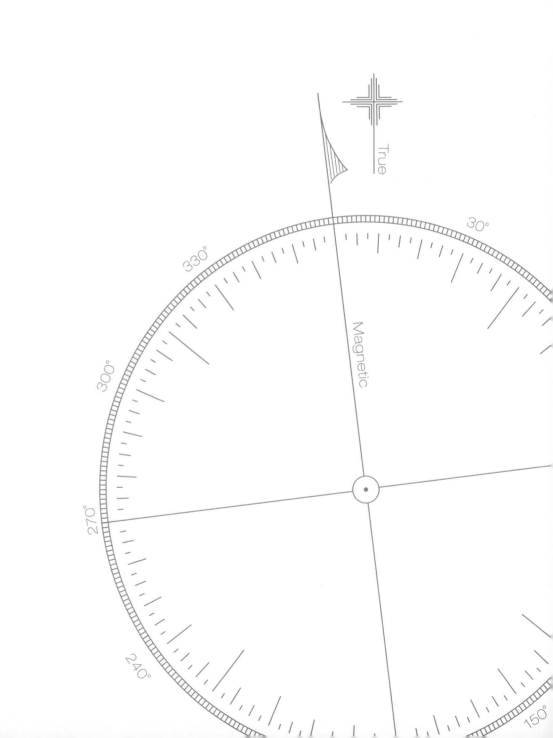

55.5°N

3°W
Ian Hamilton Finlay 1925 - 2006
Little Sparta, Lanarkshire

4°W
Rolf Roscher and Chris Rankin
The Hidden Gardens, Glasgow

James Alexander Sinclair
Mount Stuart, Isle of Bute

6°W
Peter Cool
Jura House, Isle of Jura

Ian Hamilton Finlay 1925 – 2006
Little Sparta, Lanarkshire

'The moor of routine nests the lark'

'Superior gardens are composed of glooms
and solitudes and not of plants and trees'

'Trees are preserved by manners,
not by economy wrappers'

LIGHTS

the lights of Paimpol
the lights of Concarneau
the lights of Le Conquet
the lights of Roscoff
the lights of Ouessant
the lights of Walston
shine in the rain

for Ailie

*By day Walston is a landlocked village on
the hillside opposite the author's home.*

A WATERLILY POOL
h'arbour

'Inscriptions are the best part of a garden
as decals are the best part of Airfix kits'

Ripple, n. A Fold.
A Fluting of the Liquid Element

A ROSE IS A ROSE IS A ROSE
(Gertrude Jekyll)

ARROWS ARE ARROWS ARE ARROWS
(Heraclitus)

'He Spoke Like an Axe.
Barere on Saint-Just'

'On the path of language there are wild
flowers: consonants and vowels'

Rolf Roscher and Chris Rankin
The Hidden Gardens, Glasgow

Rolf Roscher

The original brief for the Hidden Gardens was to create a space that would have 'spiritual resonance' for the communities surrounding it. The site was, at that time, an incidental patch of derelict ground – lost to the city and its inhabitants. This challenging idea prompted an investigation of the relationship between 'belief' and 'landscape'.

In the broadest terms, it could be argued that this relationship exists in two forms, which for ease of discussion we termed: the 'transported' and the 'specific'.

The 'specific': where belief is derived from place. Where a belief system has developed in response to a specific landscape – and is in effect a metaphor for that landscape. Many early cultures developed a set of beliefs that celebrate the landscape and invest it with spiritual meaning.

This is a celebration of a specific, given, landscape – it places spiritual value on a particular hill, valley or tree. The design of the Hidden Gardens celebrates the given landscape. Not hill or valley – but nursery, chimney and factory floor.

The 'transported': where a landscape is created as a metaphor for a set of beliefs. Such 'created' landscapes are often representations of idealised places from religious writings – for example the idea of the 'Paradise Garden' that is common to both Christian and Islamic tradition.

The Hidden Gardens makes reference to different traditions of garden design. But more particularly it makes reference to the traditions that were found to have resonance with local people. The aim has been to trace back common ideas and themes in these different cultural and horticultural traditions and to express them in the garden.

The Hidden Gardens celebrates the 'given' landscape alongside the cultural traditions of the people who live around it today. The garden could not be anywhere else – it has developed in direct response to the site and the local community. The design is however deliberately ambiguous, it contains layers of meaning – but may be read and experienced in many different ways.

Chris Rankin

Living in Edinburgh means one cannot fail to appreciate the importance of gardens in a city. Be they public or private, the presence and scale of the great New Town gardens form a vital component in the urban environment, not only as green spaces to relax in but as spatial components with an equivalence to the built form.

During the 20th century however, gardens suffered the same fate as the wider designed landscape. They were considered as some kind of compensation for urban life instead of being integral to how we think about city gardens and became the preserve of eccentrics and loners.

But in earlier centuries the garden played a significant role in the development of wider ideas on art, philosophy and politics. In his essay 'The Pleasure of Architecture' written in 1977 Bernard Tschumi claims that the history of garden design has led the development of urban form. 200 years previously Marc-Antoine Laugier proclaimed that whoever knows how to design a park well, will have no difficulty in tracing the plan for the building of a city.

The ground however appears to be shifting and gardens are once again being considered as important components of the urban environment. I hope that the design of the Hidden Gardens in some small way contributed to the reawakening of contemporary urban garden design in the UK.

I like the assertion of the late Ian Hamilton Finlay that a garden should not be thought of as a retreat but as an attack. It is a sentiment which I returned to whilst working on the design of the Hidden Gardens.

The aggression of the term attack may seem antithetical to the activity of garden design but I preferred to think of it as an assertion of ideas and determination in the face of lethargy and occasional antipathy. And much as Tschumi suggests that the principles of the renaissance garden were applied to the design of the squares and streets of the renaissance city, and the crescents of the 18th century city were influenced by the picturesque garden tradition, so perhaps the design of a garden like the Hidden Gardens offers an insight into the future of our contemporary cities.

Many of the ideas which underpinned the garden design have a wider currency and relevance to how we wish to design our towns and cities. Consultation was an important part of the design process and was co-ordinated brilliantly by Clare Hunter. The time taken to find out the local desires of a diverse local population, what people wanted, what kind of environment was needed in East Pollokshields contributed in many ways to our concept for the garden. The principles of re-use and re-emergence equally allowed us to retain those traces of the site's history and to find new uses and meaning for materials which might otherwise be discarded. Finally the universal and timeless quality of all gardens could not escape our attention; that the Hidden Gardens should be a place of unadulterated pleasure.

James Alexander Sinclair
Mount Stuart, Isle of Bute

Over the years I have made a lot of gardens: some large, some small; some modern, some traditional; some happy, some sad; some that worked and (to be brutally honest) some that missed. There are very few that I have felt were an absolute privilege to work on and, strangely, two of those were in Scotland. Mount Stuart, however, was the best. Seldom does a garden designer get to sink his teeth into a project where architecture and history blends so well with adventure, innovation and excitement.

I have made two gardens at Mount Stuart: the first by remodelling and replanting the Kitchen Garden originally laid out by Rosemary Verey nearly twenty years ago. The second garden was brand new and based around the startlingly modern Visitor Centre. The two are very different animals but are linked together by an exuberant use of lots and lots of plants. In the Kitchen Garden there are great swathes of perennials planted in large borders around the central pavilion. Based loosely on a colour wheel the flowers skip from blues to scalding reds through purples, pinks, greens and yellows. The Visitor Centre garden is more disciplined with long lines of grasses and spines of flowers laid out in the shape of an unfurled paper clip. This contrasts with the strong horizontal lines of the building itself.

The Butes and Mount Stuart have always been connected with gardens: the 3rd Earl helped found Kew Gardens, the Second Marquess brought Dahlias back from the New World, the Third planted the Pinetum and the Sixth brought in plants from all over Asia. The house is magnificent and the surrounding gardens are suitably diverse and diverting. I have spent many hours wandering around the gardens: both among the hustle of visitors and alone as the late sun sets across the island. The light, the island, the (occasional!) rain, the plants, the house and the sound of time passing has made the experience of working here a spine tingling pleasure.

The Visitor Centre garden
Pages 89-91

close A JOURNEY IN SCOTLAND

The Kitchen Garden. *Pages 92-93*

Peter Cool
Jura House and Garden, Isle of Jura

Jura House garden was started by the Campbells of Jura. The date on the sundial says 1812, so that is probably when the walls were built and the basic layout was created. In 1938 the Riley-Smith family bought Ardfin Estate from the Campbells.

I came here in 1976, having trained at an organic horticultural college in Holland. My original brief was to produce fruit and vegetables for Jura House and Jura Hotel. We produced enough organic vegetables to sell the surplus to the local residents.

Being aware of the potential for more exotic plants, I started to develop the borders, growing many plants from seed. The layout of the formal Victorian kitchen garden, with box and beech hedges was still intact and made a great foundation for my more informal planting style.

In 1990 Francis Riley-Smith sent me on a seed collection trip to Australia, Tasmania and New Zealand. Many of the now established plants originate from that time. They thrive here because of the Gulf Stream lapping on our shores and the use of lots of compost, seaweed and manure from our estate farm.

Slowly, as the garden became more ornamental, the visitor numbers increased and I began selling plants so we moved from vegetables and vegetable sales to visitors and plant sales.

I allow plants to do their own thing, but with a measure of control, so allowing self-seeding and spreading of some plants, while controlling and weeding others – it creates an informal style.

I consider myself very lucky to have the opportunity to live on this beautiful island and to have been given the freedom to create this garden.

close A JOURNEY IN SCOTLAND

close A JOURNEY IN SCOTLAND

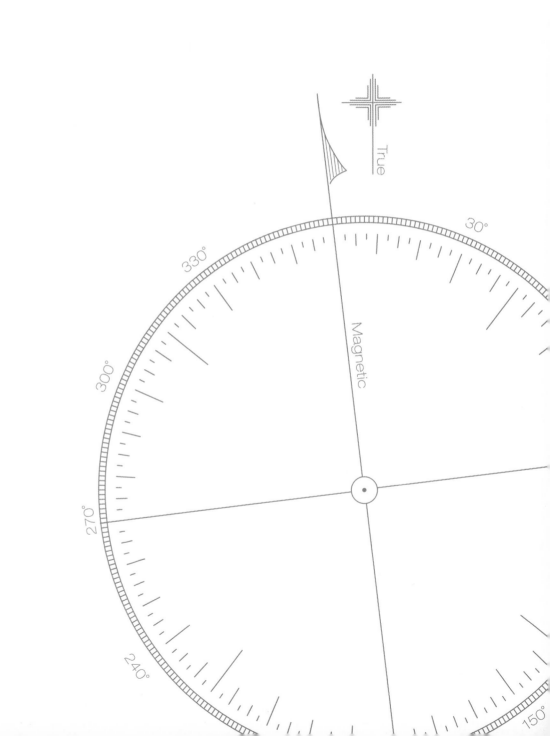

56°N

2°W
Catherine Erskine & Elliot Forsyth
Cambo House, Fife

4°W
Jinny Blom
Corrour Lodge Gardens, by Fort William

Niall Manning & Alastair Morton
Dun Ard, Stirlingshire

6°W
Penelope Hobhouse Hon.D.Litt. M.A.
The Monks Garden, an island in the
Inner Hebrides

Catherine Erskine & Elliot Forsyth
Cambo House, Fife

Catherine Erskine

We are very lucky at Cambo, living on the coast of Fife, often described as a beggar's mantle fringed with gold, with fertile, free draining soil and a good climate, missing the excessive rainfall of the west and with dry, sunny days.

Carefully chosen by the original designers of the garden, it is the wonderful setting of the 2½ acre walled garden gently sloping up from each side of the Cambo burn and creating a protected micro-climate that gives us the opportunity to grow such a wide range of plants. With high walls and surrounded by mature trees planted by previous generations we have maximum shelter from the bitter east winds coming in from the sea.

Our aims have always been to build on this wonderful setting creating a place that is inspiring and up-lifting in all seasons – an oasis of calm and beauty. Someone said to me recently, 'The problem with walled gardens is the corners'. I had never thought of this before but it is true in that the walls dictate the shape of the garden and can dominate if you allow them to. We have designed the plantings at Cambo to draw the visitors inwards – we have moved away from the functional geometric shapes to meandering paths through dense plantings and created a feeling of 'rooms' in the garden.

We continually experiment with the new – different ways of planting, a new palette of plants – but we also retain traditional elements and plants, the two blending to create what we regard as a delightfully unique whole. Nevertheless, what is ostensibly an ornamental garden remains a working garden, still providing the house with flowers and produce throughout the year.

I would never want to feel that we had finished and were only maintaining the garden. There is always a new plan or re-development on the go and that is what makes the garden vibrant and keeps us all motivated.

Elliott Forsyth

My work draws on the natural landscape, the fields, hedgerows, coastline and the constantly changing skies of the East Neuk. Naturalistic planting combines nature and art theory to produce borders which emphasise colour and form.

At Cambo we want to create a rhythm and unity in the planting. It is finding a balance between planting to a theme that has a recognisable tone though the garden, while at the same time using plants to their full effect. To me every plant says something totally different. Grasses are an integral aspect in the creation of a difused naturalistic effect. The way they move, combine, and catch the light helps invoke a sense of nature.

close A JOURNEY IN SCOTLAND

close A JOURNEY IN SCOTLAND

Jinny Blom
Corrour Lodge Gardens, by Fort William

The call to visit Corrour for the first time came at Halloween in the year 2000. Arriving off the sleeper train from London into a spectacular Highland landscape of bronze, rust and dun; its fiery autumn colours were breathtaking.

The invitation had been extended to transform the landscaping around the eleven miles of Loch road and also around the newly commissioned lodge, designed by the eminent architect Moshe Safdie. The new lodge was being built on the footprint of an impressive Victorian lodge that had burned to the ground in the 1940's. Thus began a long term and entirely unique project.

The estate had been in gentle decline for some time as timber prices had slumped and the nearest viable road was many miles away down forest tracks, making the sale of the plantations uneconomic. This fact informed much of the rationale behind the new landscaping. When the original Victorian lodge had been built it was the heyday of industry, wealth poured out of Glasgow. Navvies were brought from the building of the railways and vast labour forces set to work creating extravagant gardens of boulders, pools, networks of paths, cottages and taming the volatile burns to power the estate. The then owner, Sir John Stirling Maxwell, planted thousands of trees as an experiment in Highland planting and formed the Forestry Commission in its wake. An avid plant hunter, he planted an astonishing secret Rhododendron plantation at this improbable altitude.

This level of endeavour cannot be replicated these days and the thrust of contemporary landscaping on this scale is firmly in the direction of ecology and sustainability. It was agreed that the landscape would be designed to need minimal human management and use, as far as possible, locally indigenous species. The spread of plant disease is rife as there is so much traffic involved in the business yet the estate is clean and pure and miraculously free of it.

With such an astonishing building the gardens could not compete, instead they have become 'anti gardens'. I created a matrix of seed, grasses, trees and shrubs of local appropriateness and threaded them right up to the base of the building, lapping like waves against this alien cliff. The vestiges of the Victorian garden were restored, rather in the manner of an old Roman mosaic, and woven into the whole. The reminiscences of the Victorian gardens were threaded into the wilder plantings: Swamp lilies, Himalayan cowslips, huge Cardiocrinums and exotic ferns that would have graced the best Victorian gardens and spoken of the owners erudition in plant hunting circles, have naturalized and pop up haphazardly through the birch copses and at the feet of Scots Pines. Trees tap at the windows of the Lodge; creepers are beginning to cover its walls; it is gradually melding with its environment.

A venture of this size is never complete and each year adjustments and additions are made, thinking develops and new information is greedily consumed. Gratifyingly, nature is returning, deer numbers are controlled so natural regeneration can take place and overgrazing is held in check. A gentle blooming is occurring in this extraordinary and evocative place.

The road to Corrour
Page 118

Sculpture by Anthony Gormley
Page 119

close A JOURNEY IN SCOTLAND

Niall Manning & Alastair Morton
Dun Ard, Stirlingshire

We started gardening here 20 years ago in what was an open field. A plan was drawn up at the outset, responding to the site and its place in the wider landscape. We were keen to develop a garden with vivid contrasts: a feeling of enclosure and wide views out; a strong geometrical framework with exuberant planting and meadows. We were particularly keen to explore the contrast between a formal design and the views out to hills and moorland.

We appear to be in an age when the subject of garden-making and gardening "has been reduced to the outdoor equivalent of DIY" (Tim Richardson, Arcadian Friends 2008). "The spirit of place" is seldom considered and basic questions about individual gardens are rarely asked: What is it for? and What does it mean? A useful corrective to much writing about garden design would be the chapter headings in Douglas Swinscow's book The Mystic Garden: A Symbolic Journey, Expectation & Invitation, Surprise, Boundaries, Joy & Mystery, Perseverance, Knowledge, Finding the Way, Fulfilment, Harmony, Awakening, Serenity and Illumination.

We see our garden as a place to walk in, work in and experience in all weathers and seasons. We find many gardens overtidy and overwrought. The organic production of vegetables and fruit is a central part of what we do here. It is a loved place, a healing place and also fun.

Penelope Hobhouse Hon.D.Litt. MA.
The Monks Garden, an Island in the Inner Hebrides

This small walled garden is on a windswept island in the Inner Hebrides. It was designed for clients who live on the coast north of Boston across the Atlantic. While north-east United States has very cold winters, the island is washed by the warm Gulf Stream and has no frost, making it possible to grow a number of tender plants, especially some from New Zealand which are resistant to salt spray and storms. The principle hazard is wind which often reaches gale force and frequently changes direction, creating pockets of turbulence under the walls. There are no trees, except for a few stunted willows, growing on the island, but the garden is protected from the north by the Ben, its highest hill.

My approach was to make a network of hedges in an asymmetrical pattern to avoid wind funnels and I used privet that grows so well on the east end of Long Island. For the first few years these were wrapped up in burlap to prevent wind scorch but are now thriving. The compartments created by the hedges provide almost wind-free spaces in which shrubs, perennials, herbs and vegetables can thrive. One 'room' reflects the planting done by 14th century monks who owned the garden attached to their priory. The island was the first land visited by Saint Columba on his way from Ireland to Iona. Another garden compartment takes its theme from the plants used by Gertrude Jekyll when she laid out a garden on the Holy Island of Lindisfarne in the early 20th century. It has salt-resistant silver-leaved plants.

Elsewhere there is mixed planting of rugosa roses, peonies, New Zealand shrubs and bulbs all of which survive the rugged conditions, and seem to enjoy the Atlantic storms. The clients look after the garden impeccably.

close A JOURNEY IN SCOTLAND

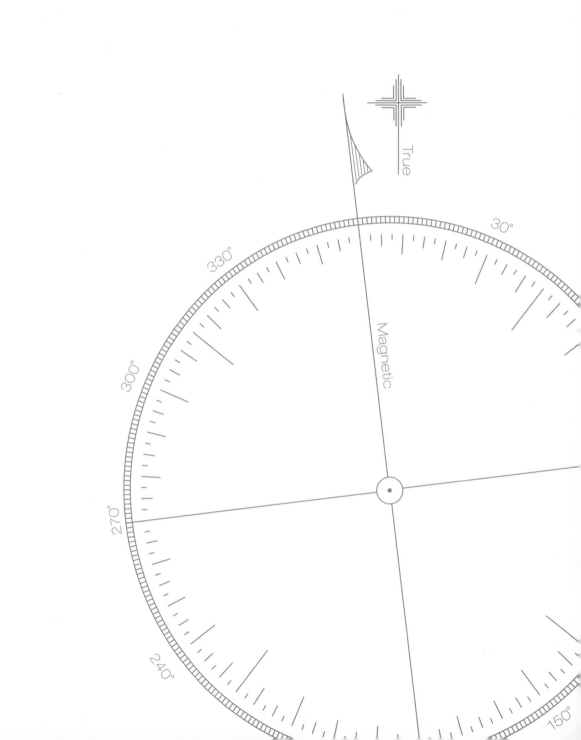

57°N

2°W

Mary Ann Crichton Maitland
Daluaine, Aberdeenshire

Dr. Thomas Smith
Rubislaw Den North, Aberdeen

3°W

Angelika, Dowager Countess Cawdor
Cawdor Castle and Gardens, Nairn

4°W

Gerald Laing
Kinkell, Ross & Cromarty

Mary Ann Crichton Maitland
Daluaine, Aberdeenshire

Daluaine, originally a manse, was acquired nearly 40 years ago. Untended for many years, the small early 18th century walled garden is now a riot of colourful herbaceous plants. Facing south on a gentle slope, it is protected from the harsh North Eastern climate by a stand of fine old beech trees on the North side.

The glebe land below the house was added 12 years ago. From an exposed docken and nettle patch, it has become a 4 acre arboretum on a steep slope above the river Bogie. A wide variety of trees and shrubs have been planted to blend together, particularly for their leaf shape and autumn colours. Many paths have been cut into the slope to enable this area to be viewed at all angles. Sorbus, betula and acer abound.

This is a garden for all seasons. It has evolved over the years with no particular plan. I am an avid collector of plants, but seldom buy on impulse and tend to hunt for something for a particular area or idea.

Nothing is cut down until the Spring, as winters can be severe. The plants are protected by their own leaves and stalks and add interest in frosty weather and shelter for the many birds who love this garden.

Many visitors come now and it is a pleasure to share it.

Dr. Thomas Smith
Rubislaw Den North, Aberdeen

This garden has been in a constant state of reconfiguration during the last few decades. The changes continue. They result from how I change whilst living and working in North East Scotland.

The landscape has been a major influence, particularly the Scottish mountains under snow. But also the lowlands of Perthshire and Aberdeenshire with the beautiful valleys of Dee and Don with their hinterland of rolling rich farmland and coastal fringe of rock and sand.

Equally important has been my experience of the people and culture of Aberdeen and Aberdeenshire. It has seemed to me that there was a respect for learning, which helped make a good climate for the scholarship pursued in the university. This was enhanced by the memory of illustrious predecessors such as the great Scottish philosopher Sir Thomas Reid who was born near Aberdeen and the greatest Scottish Natural Philosopher James Clark Maxwell who worked here.

Gardens are experienced holistically, but this experience is most rewarding when the whole is composed of many parts. One part will usually be a concern for the plants as living entities with their differing colours and forms. One will be an aesthetic response to colour and pattern in the different garden areas and in the garden as a whole. Another, especially for those who love the mountains, can be the response to sculptured spaces resulting from the contours of the land and from the vertical planting. It is always stimulating to look at gardens and landscapes in this way. However an intellectual response can also be pleasurable. So the knowledgeable spectator might consider where the plants grow wild, their taxonomic and phylogeny etc. Also the garden structures and sculptures may suggest something of a garden's relation to the encompassing world. Thus in this garden, a ruined 'observatory' with a sky 'telescope' of narrow poplars elicits an experience of the garden as embedded in space-time. Further sculptures with quantum mechanic and relativity equations recall to the spectator other hidden aspects of the mystery in which both gardener and garden live and so the total experience is enriched.

Gardens can also feed the spirit. They can be for contemplation, for meditation, for imagination, for poetry and for philosophic reflection. These moods are nurtured by the planting, views, seats etc. In this garden they are also influenced by philosophic and spiritual inscriptions. (In the nearby garden made in 1604 in Edzell Castle, one can still see the sculptured panels in which Sir David Lindsay alludes to the learning and spirituality of his world with panels representing the Planetary Deities, the Liberal Arts and the Cardinal Virtues.)

Both the making and the viewing of the garden landscape can be an act of artistic creation in which the gardener or garden visitor explores and engages with the richness of the contemporaneous world at every level. It is an active dialogue in which the world, particularly its plants, are as important as the action of the gardener or the garden visitor.

close A JOURNEY IN SCOTLAND

Angelika, Dowager Countess Cawdor
Cawdor Castle and Gardens, Nairn

The Castle dates from the 14th century and has been lived in by the family in a direct line ever since. The Cawdors have been keen gardeners over generations and enthusiastic planstsmen, passionate about trees. The sycamore trees on the front lawn were planted by Sir Archibald Campbell in the mid 18th century. The limes in front of the Castle were planted circa 1717.

Cawdor is fortunate in having three gardens. The oldest garden north east of the Castle was enclosed with walls and bastions in 1620 and was cultivated in the old fashioned manner with soft fruit, flowers, vegetables and an orchard. Hugh, the 6th Earl Cawdor opened the Castle to the public in 1976. The Walled Garden became a favourite with visitors but unfortunately they considered it as a free supermarket and would pull up the carrots, take the onions, etc. until finally the head gardener threatened to resign because he had found a local vicar under the strawberry nets. Hugh then decided it was time to make changes. In 1981 it was replanted and now has a holly maze and symbolic gardens representing Paradise, the Earth and the Garden of Eden, planted by Angelika, the Dowager Lady Cawdor.

The Flower Garden to the south of the Castle was laid out a full century later, again in the old style. In 1850 Lady Cawdor added the oval rose beds edged with lavender, which are still there today. This garden was originally designed for enjoyment in late summer and autumn, with great herbaceous borders.

The Wild Garden on the stream bank of the Cawdor Burn gives another contrast with rhododendrons and spring bulbs as well as bamboos, ferns and gunnera manicata.

Cawdor Castle and Gardens are open to the public every day from 1st May until the second Sunday in October.

close A JOURNEY IN SCOTLAND

close A JOURNEY IN SCOTLAND

Gerald Laing
Kinkell, Ross and Cromarty

My garden is wild, sophisticated, and kept on a long lead. Gus, my gardener and friend, acts more as a referee in the continuous and ruthless Battle of the Flowers than a policeman trying to keep order. It is a more virtuous and humane role, and requires far more sensitivity. The sculpture which punctuates the text of the garden makes references that both complement and compete with the living vegetation. Some of it is in permanent residence, and some merely pausing before its journey to elsewhere begins.

close A JOURNEY IN SCOTLAND

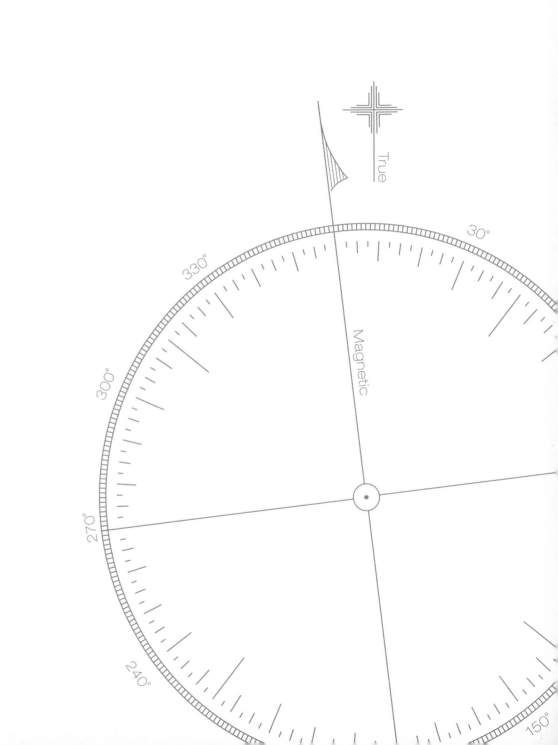

close A JOURNEY IN SCOTLAND

58°N
3°W

Xa Tollemache
Dunbeath, Caithness

Xa Tollemache
Dunbeath,Caithness

With the winds getting up to 100 mph and coming from almost any angle; with the salt spray lightly settling on the plants on a bad day; and with it taking almost the whole day to reach from my home in Suffolk, Dunbeath was a very challenging project. But it is such an inspirational place and never ceases to amaze and delight. With its spectacular entrance and position, this great white castle, perched on rocks out to sea and the sycamores bending in reverence to the wind, can take your breath away (and this can mean literally). The complete enthusiasm and hard work of the owners and gardeners made the resurrection and recreation of this walled garden pure pleasure.

The landscape in Caithness is massive. Not mountainous and dramatic like the West coast, but open and rolling. It feels like you are cruising along on top of the world; the scale is big and that is why Dunbeath works so well, everything is in proportion to what is going on around it.

close A JOURNEY IN SCOTLAND

close A JOURNEY IN SCOTLAND

close A JOURNEY IN SCOTLAND

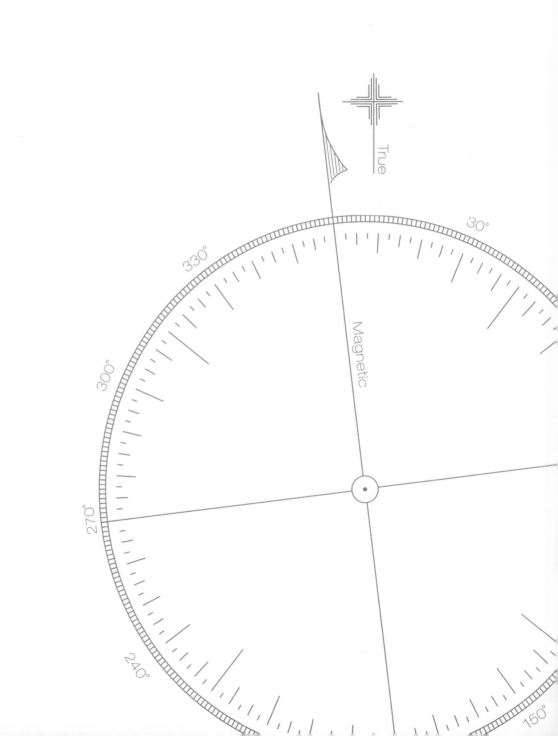

30°

330°

300°

270°

240°

150°

True

Magnetic

60°N

'close' exhibition
Bonhoga Gallery, Shetland
14 February 2009 – 15 March 2009

www.shetlandarts.org

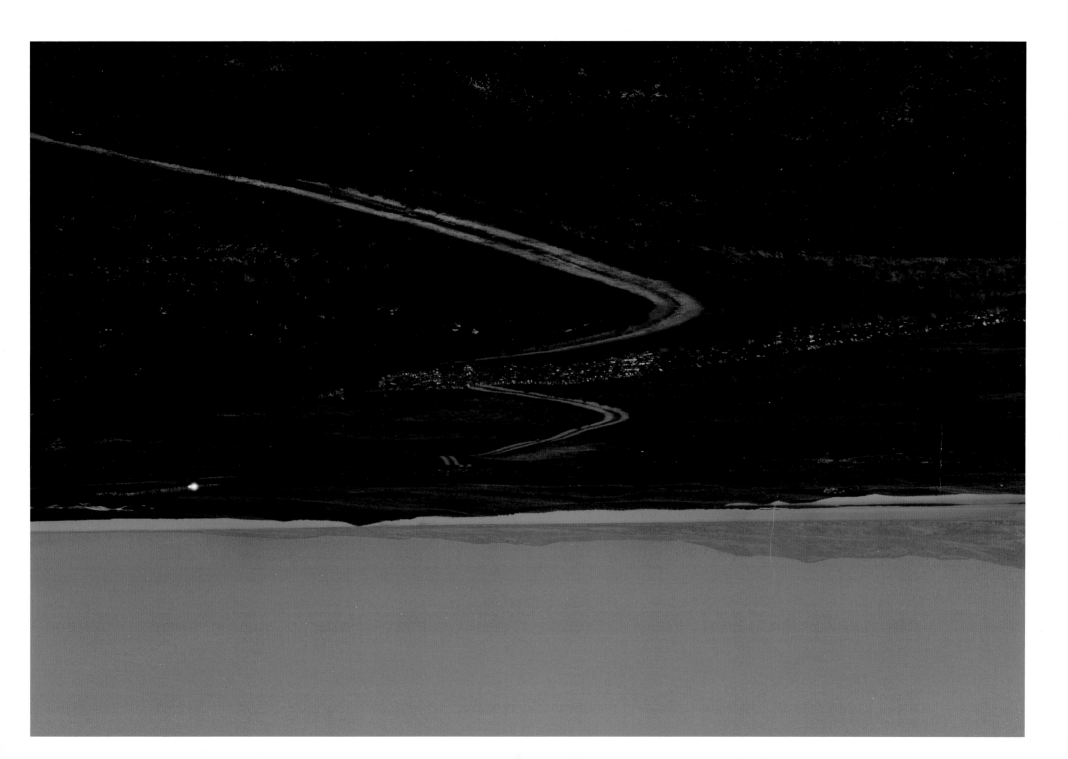

Allan Pollok-Morris
Acknowledgements

'Thankyou for leting us in you'r gardens'

These words taken from The Hidden Gardens in Glasgow say it all (page 86).
It is a very undervalued gift for someone to open a special, personal space to the public
or the critical eye of a documentary professional. Although the last thing the owners or
designers are looking for is gratitude, I must say a huge thank you for their hospitality
and the opportunity to share these works with a wider audience.

I am very grateful to all the contributors to this collection. Some of the writers are published internationally and it has been very rewarding to bring them together for this Scottish project. Thank you very much to Sir Roy Strong FSA., FSRL. for his foreword.

I must thank Pia Simig for choosing the late Ian Hamilton Finlays' words and the selection of images for the section on Little Sparta. Thanks to Jessie Sheeler and Richard Ingleby for their help with the initial research.

Andy Goldsworthy and Eric J Sawden's help with the project in very demanding timescales has been very much appreciated.

Many thanks to Charles Jencks for all his help, particularly the use of his imagery of the Edinburgh Landform and Inverness Maggie's Centre – and also to Maggie's Centres themselves for their help with this.

Thanks to Penelope Hobhouse and Alec Finlay for helping in a variety of ways, that have also spilled over into other projects.

James Alexander Sinclair has been a great help with the project since the early stages including his advice on the wider aspect of gardens in Scotland.

Jinny Blom's work at Corrour was a welcome addition to the project, less than a month before the exhibition and catalogue went to press. Unfortunately I didn't have time to wait for the kind of good day I would hope for and it is a credit to Jinny's design and the natural landscape that the images worked so well in a bad light. The timescales meant we were unable to get together and so the portrait by Virginia Liberatore was gratefully received.

Mairi Gillies, the curator at the Royal Botanic Gardens Edinburgh had to show nearly double the amount of work that was foreseen at the beginning of the project, not that we didn't share the same excitement at how the subject grew in scope, but it is a challenging task for any curator to work with a set space in that context – thanks Mairi.

Thanks in advance to Mary Smith, the curator for the Shetland Arts Organisation for travelling some of the prints and words on to Shetland in 2009.

I have to thank a number of my clients from Europe, Russia and the USA, for indirectly funding the project by publishing articles covering the subjects in this collection. One of those clients, Chris Young from the Royal Horticultural Society Journal 'The Garden', also leant his eye in the final stages of the catalogue production – thanks very much for that.

Thanks to Eric Joakim from Phase 1 of Denmark who has helped with the equipment needed for both night and day imagery. Likewise the many people at Printer Trento in Italy for their help with the catalogue production.

I have to say thanks to Tara Harris who had a huge task on her hands with the prints for the exhibition and also The Creative Place for their support with the mounting of the prints.

Elle Moss, the founder of Drew Creative can't be thanked enough for her support in the catalogue design, coping with a fast moving target and, in my opinion, hitting the right note from the word go. A few other friends I must thank are Justina Burnett for her ongoing help with retouching and printing of the portraits and texts, Will Atkinson for his help with the writing, Keith & Jen Dyer, Andrew Watson and Janet Hardy and of course my Mum, Caitlin and our kids for their support and company along the way.

At the end of the day a big thanks has to go to the gardeners, paid & volunteer workers and local organisations who contribute to the maintenance of places like those in this collection.